FZ

FZ

Tom Tierney

Florenz Ziegfeld

1920s costume ball

PLATE 1

Do not cut out
white areas between
body and arms.

Tom Tierney

Anna Held
A Parlor Match (1896)

1896 vaudeville tour

PLATE 2

Do not cut out
white areas between
arm and body.

AH

AH

The Little Duchess (1901)

Papa's Wife (1899)

PLATE 3

Cut hat along
dotted line.

LL

LL

Tom Tierney

Lillian Lorraine
Ziegfeld Follies of 1912

"Any Old Time at All"
Ziegfeld Follies of 1918

PLATE 4

Cut hat along
dotted line.

Tom Tierney

Billie Burke
Jerry (1914)

The Amazons (1913)

PLATE 5

Do not cut out
white areas between
arms and body.

Rose Briar (1922)

The Wizard of Oz (1939)

BB

BB

PLATE 6

Do not cut out
white areas between
arms and body.

Tom Tierney

Marilyn Miller
Smiles (1930)

Sally (1920)

PLATE 7

Cut hat along
dotted line.

FB

Fannie Brice (1)
"Rose of Washington Square"
Ziegfeld Follies of 1920

Fannie Brice (2)
Ziegfeld Follies of 1910

PLATE 8

FB1

FB2

Ziegfeld Follies of 1910

As "Baby Snooks,"
Ziegfeld Follies of 1936

PLATE 9

Do not cut out
white areas between
arms and body.

AP

Ann Pennington
Ziegfeld Follies of 1913

Ziegfeld Follies of 1916

PLATE 10

Ziegfeld Follies of 1924

Ziegfeld Follies of 1924

PLATE 11

Ziegfeld Follies of 1927

Clare Luce
No Foolin' (1926)

PLATE 12

Do not cut out
white areas between
arms and body.

CL

Ziegfeld Follies of 1927

PLATE 13

Helen Morgan
Showboat (1927)

Showboat (1927)

PLATE 14

"Ziegfeld Beauty"
Ziegfeld Follies of 1924

Ziegfeld Follies of 1923

PLATE 15